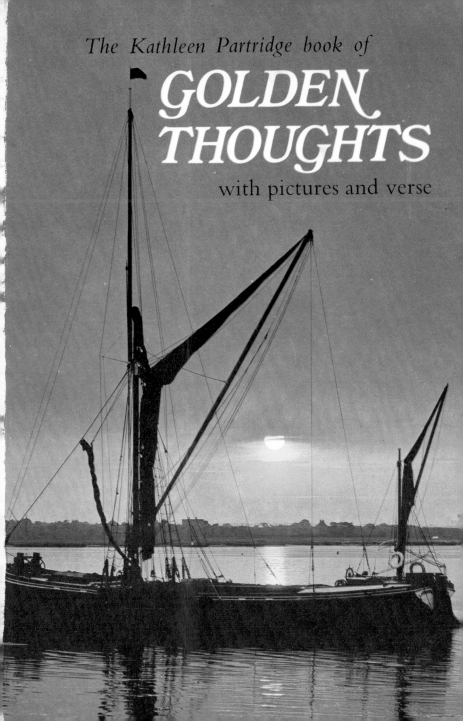

The Kathleen Partridge book of

GOLDEN
THOUGHTS

with pictures and verse

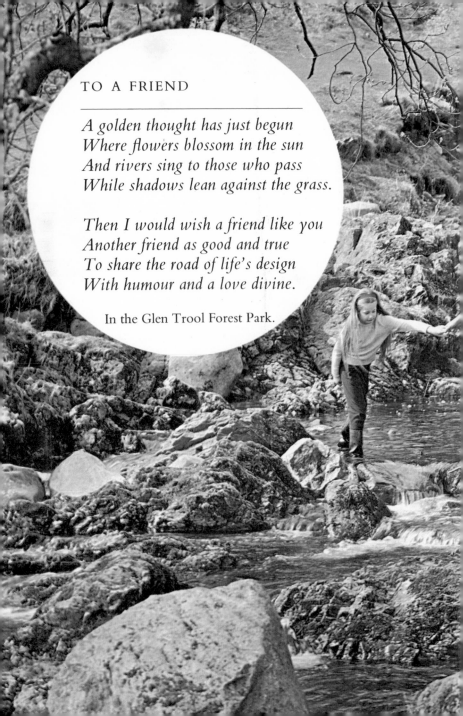

TO A FRIEND

A golden thought has just begun
Where flowers blossom in the sun
And rivers sing to those who pass
While shadows lean against the grass.

Then I would wish a friend like you
Another friend as good and true
To share the road of life's design
With humour and a love divine.

In the Glen Trool Forest Park.

Turn back the page, the page of time
To the olden days of maypoles and mime
To a white horse carved on an old green hill
With a mason's art and a carpenter's skill.

To beautiful churches in ancient glory
And stained glass windows that tell a story
Turn back the page, recapture grace
And try to live at a quieter pace.

Many grand English houses take the title of Abbey from ancient religious foundations on the same site. *Opposite*: Barton Abbey, Oxfordshire. *Above*: the romantic ruins of Tintern Abbey, Monmouthshire.

ONLY A PETAL

Only a leaf in the morning dew
Or hole in the fence where a rose climbs through
The song of the sea or the sunset's kiss
Life is worth living for this.

Only the smile of the child next door
Or news from a friend on a distant shore
Though the rest of the day has gone amiss
Life is worth living for this.

Only a petal pale and pink
With memories sweet to form a link
With past or present times of bliss
Life is worth living for this.

Cactus lovers lavish the care on their specimens that
others spend on their pets. *Left*: the profusely bloomed
Epiphyllum. *Above*: a rare and delicate foreign plant –
Dimorphotheca 'Jucunda'.

TOLL OF TIME

Time takes its toll
And those we love grow dearer with the years
Of no avail are past regrets
Life has no time for tears.

Live and laugh and help each other
Whether working or at leisure
To be happy, loved and needed
Is life's greatest source of pleasure.

Opposite: Castle Howard, Yorkshire, a magnificent eighteenth-century mansion (by Vanbrugh) set in acres of parkland. Equally grandiose is the Duke of Devonshire's stately home, Chatsworth House in Derbyshire.

SUNBEAMS

If all the golden sunbeams
Could be gathered in to spend
With all the loving thoughts and deeds
When day was at an end.

And tied with strings of laughter
On wings of wonder born
They'd beautify the eventide
And bless tomorrow's dawn.

Northern Ireland's beautiful scenery is represented by these two pictures of its most famous features. *Opposite*: rapidly cooling lava formed the pillars of the Giant's Causeway. *Above*: the Mourne Mountains.

ANOTHER DAY

Old cares are like the morning mist
Before the rising sun
But it is true, the blue shines through
Before the day is done.

And then the fears of yesteryears
Go rolling down the lane
Another day, smiles on its way
And life begins again.

Left: a lonely, deserted crofter's cottage stands by a loch
at Beinn na Cille, in Ardgour in the Western Highlands
of Scotland. Pink willowherb makes an attractive picture
at Loch Lubnaig.

Peace and the flowing river of life
Offer us hope and a little song
A sense of comfort and ease from strife
Whenever the toils of life are strong.

And over the hills where the views are kind
A feeling of freedom is waiting there
A solace of heart and soul and mind
Out on the grass in the open air.

The Swallow Falls *(left)*, at Betws-y-Coed, are one of the
great scenic attractions of Wales. The picture above shows
another Welsh cascade, on the River Rheidol in mid-
Wales.

SOMEBODY'S GARDEN

Someone planned this garden
From the beauty in his soul
And kept his spirits joyful
As he worked towards this goal.

Breathing sunshine from the flowers
And wisdom from the leaves
To offer comfort to the sad
And peace to the heart that grieves.

Welford-on-Avon, Warwickshire.

BLOSSOMING SMILE

Nature's loveliness would pall
If flowers had no scent at all
For beauty lifeless, stands apart
Without the fragrance in the heart.

A maiden might a goddess be
Perfect in grace and symmetry
Yet stand unnoticed for a while
Without the beauty of a smile.

The rare oxlip *(opposite)* may look like a cowslip to the uninitiated, but to the botanist there is a world of difference. *Above*: an arrangement of roses in a pottery vase.

A joyful manner of living
Is a tune for the day to start
The pleasure in doing and giving
Brings peace to the happy heart.

With courage for daily duty
And patience when problems arise
Thankful for bounty and beauty
Living in ways that are wise.

Flora Macdonald was held prisoner in Dunstaffanage Castle *(above)*, a stronghold of the Campbells at the mouth of Loch Etive. *Right*: a Scottish regimental piper in full regalia.

He is more than a pet. He is more than a friend.
 He's a reason for living on which we depend.
With his head on one side and his paw held
 aloft, our firmest reproval grows suddenly soft.
He meets us, he greets us, enslaved from the
 start, when he nuzzles our hand as he tugs at
 our heart.

Dogs have an appeal all their own, whether it be the soulful melancholy of an English Setter *(left)* or the mischief in the eyes of these Dachshund pups.

DREAM COTTAGE

We picture a country cottage
Set in a country lane
Scented with old fashioned flowers
And sheltered against the rain.

Old timbers and quiet windows
With a beautiful garden view
Where the shadows play in the evening
And the morning sun filters through.

It's a dream that can make us happy
When we live in a busy part
Dreaming the dream of 'OUR COTTAGE'
And keeping the hope in our heart.

Vicar's Cottage, Aymestry, Herefordshire.

WISDOM OF THE WAVES

When the ships are safe in harbour
And the boats are anchored tight
When the sun gleams on the water
There is not a fairer sight.

The lonely heart is comforted
The troubled mind set free
As if the cares of all the world
Were sailing out to sea.

Translucent seas of brilliant blue are the dream of any holidaymaker whether he is addicted to the charm of Mevagissey with its quaint harbour *(left)*, or the sun-scorched beaches of Guernsey *(above)*.

Horses have a traditional hold on an Englishman who may enjoy showjumping *(above)* or parading through country lanes in fancy-dress in a four-in-hand *(right)*. This stage-coach is often to be seen in East Anglia.

FRIENDSHIP

Old friends are like old shoes
They are so fitted to the years
They know our highest efforts
And discern our secret fears.

They've walked with us and waited
When we aimed for better things
Through embarrassment or glory
Poor as paupers, proud as kings.

And though for various reasons
Shoes wear out and friendships end
We lose part of our lives
Each time we quarrel with a friend.

Is it an angel's secret tears
In the heart of a rose when the dew appears?
Or the scroll that curls at the petal's edge
That talks of love and a lover's pledge?

Or is it the perfume, deep and sweet
Where the loveliest hours of the summer meet
To lighten the heart and to ease the woes
And make us live for the love of a rose?

So many different species of rose exist today that the breeder of a new variety may find the choice of a name difficult. *Left*: 'Silver Lining'. *Above*: 'Albertine'.

WORLD PROBLEMS

When happy do not close your eyes
To other nations woes and sighs
Though healthy, not too proud to see
Another's disability.

Let pageantry be fine and wise
With music set to sympathise
While wealth and comfort serve to stress
World problems and a child's distress.

Changing the Guard at Buckingham Palace.

GLINT OF GOLD

In every humdrum day
There is a little glint of gold
A purpose in the living
That is lovely to behold.

A reason for existence
In the dark – a glowing ember
That lights the dullest duty
With a moment to remember.

The connoisseur finds delight in noticing the different styles of cottage architecture. They may vary from the eccentricity of a pantile roof in Sussex *(left)* to tidy Suffolk thatch *(above)*.

WHERE GOD IS

Upon the hill a Norman tower
Among the trees a spire
And cuddled down amid the town
A lych gate to admire.

A cathedral in the city
Or a meeting house of prayer
Each village street, or green retreat
Proclaims that God is there.

The country inn is an essential part of our English heritage
– both socially and architecturally. These examples are at
Bishop's Tawton, Devon *(above)* and Chilham, Kent.

From the old church, organ music floats
To the lazy lapping of little boats
With perky sails and painted hulls
And over it all the squeal of gulls.

Above the harbour, bustling about
The world comes in and the world goes out
By way of a bridge – the latest kind
Created and built by a master mind.

Polperro *(left)* is an old-world Cornish fishing village *par excellence*. Its beauty attracts many artists. *Above*: the spectacular Avon Gorge and Bridge near Bristol.

Narrow traffic-free cobbled streets lined by quaint cottages give Clovelly *(above)* its timeless beauty. Proximity to London seldom deprives the old cottages of Surrey *(right)* of their rare charm.

SLEEP TIGHT

In between the dimpled hills
Along a leafy lane
A pretty cottage slumbers
In the sunshine and the rain.

The roses ramble round it
Where the apple trees bend low
And good folk live in harmony
While fashions come and go.

The place where love is waiting
In the way that God designed
When someone mentions 'HOME'
This is the place that comes to mind.

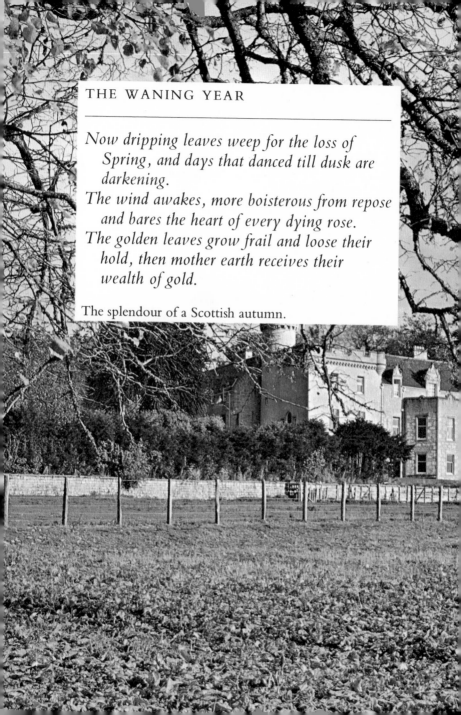

THE WANING YEAR

Now dripping leaves weep for the loss of
  Spring, and days that danced till dusk are
  darkening.
The wind awakes, more boisterous from repose
  and bares the heart of every dying rose.
The golden leaves grow frail and loose their
  hold, then mother earth receives their
  wealth of gold.

The splendour of a Scottish autumn.

The world a sorry place would be
Without a river running free
Between the meadows and the hills
With water for the farms and mills.

And pastures green lack something too
Without a river running through
With dipping ducks and swans afloat
Where men keep young who sail a boat.

An island race has a special regard for boats and in England few people can resist the sight of a sail. *Above*: boating on the Norfolk Broads; *opposite*: Christchurch, Hampshire.

TO LIFT THE HEART

Think of a lovely landscape
If ever you droop with despair
Picture the perfumed pathways
The dells and the arbours there.

Sit in a shady corner
Or lounge on a sunny slope
Where nature brings you contentment
And God will offer you hope.

The quiet, remote fishing village of New Quay (*left*) is in Cardiganshire in mid-Wales. Weathered sandstone gives Ladran Bay in Devon its character and beauty.

This is the day to wake and say
Happy the heart that is merry in May.
Gather contentment as you pass
Green and serene, the colour of grass.

To be awake when blossoms break
And sunbeams smile for someone's sake
The views so free, so much to see
The best of summer yet to be.

The beauty of Britain often depends on the wealth of wild flowers growing in strategic places. *Left*: bluebells in Nithsdale, Scotland. *Above*: rhododendrons in the Vale of Ffestiniog, Wales.

REMEMBERING

Never a day runs to an end
Without some kindness from a friend.
Without remembering the name
Of one we love who stays the same.

To doubt the love of such a one
Would be to disbelieve the sun
A lack of faith, that stays awake
Doubting that the dawn will break.

The village pond and green afford a place for relaxation at Midhurst, Sussex *(above)*. *Right*: Llanfrothen is a small village near Portmadoc in North Wales.

HIGH HOPES

May your hopes run clear
As the waters of life
And high as the shining blue
And all the love
That you gave to life
Come back on the tide to you.

May the colour of dreams
That dry your tears
Be gold as the morning glow
Bringing a blessing along the years
To the dearest people you know.

The harbour at Tenby, Pembrokeshire.

AUTUMN TINTS

Out on the common the bracken is turning
From green and yellow to bronze and gold
The flames of autumn are bright and burning
Over the hills where the clouds unfold.

And there will be fragrance from autumn showers
And morning sunshine to gleam and glisten
Scattering light on the blazing flowers
Where man may prattle and God will listen.

Above: Burnham Beeches, Buckinghamshire, are woods
purchased nearly a century ago by the City of London.
Opposite: Cotswold village of Tredington, Warwickshire.

Out on the common the bracken is turning
From green and yellow to bronze and gold
The flames of autumn are bright and burning
Over the hills where the clouds unfold.

And there will be fragrance from autumn showers
And morning sunshine to gleam and glisten
Scattering light on the blazing flowers
Where man may prattle and God will listen.

Above: Burnham Beeches, Buckinghamshire, are woods purchased nearly a century ago by the City of London. *Opposite*: Cotswold village of Tredington, Warwickshire.

There are many places of outstanding beauty in southern
Scotland. In the picture above the sun sets below the hills
of Bute. The view was taken from Largs, Ayrshire.
Opposite: the Bull Ring Centre, Birmingham, at night.

SUNSET

A golden shaft of sunlight
Makes a pathway to the sea
As if an angel host
Had walked into eternity

A blessing and a beauty
Never quite so fine before
That lights the sky at sunset
From horizon to the shore

And then we know that God is good
Whatever man may do.
A sign of love shines up above
And HOPE *is born anew.*

Most people will have few occasions to meet the timid field mouse *(opposite)* face to face, but the mare with her foal is fortunately still an endearing part of the country scene.

DINNERTIME

No sweeter sight to ease the soul
Than meadows with a horse and foal
Trampling where they love to be
Near by the shelter of a tree.

Slender forelocks flashed with white
Where yellow buttercups are bright
Tender eyes and velvet nose
Whereon the wind of heaven blows.

Who roams the countryside will know
The secret sights that do not show
But to the country lover's soul
What dearer than a horse and foal?

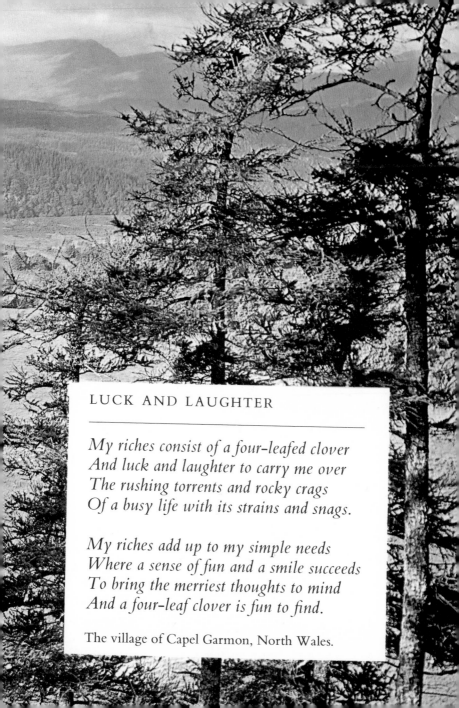

LUCK AND LAUGHTER

My riches consist of a four–leafed clover
And luck and laughter to carry me over
The rushing torrents and rocky crags
Of a busy life with its strains and snags.

My riches add up to my simple needs
Where a sense of fun and a smile succeeds
To bring the merriest thoughts to mind
And a four-leaf clover is fun to find.

The village of Capel Garmon, North Wales.

Create if you can a lovelier thing
In sheen and shade than a butterfly's wing
So many colours brightly blended
Into a life so quickly ended.

Only a day of joy and duty
To give the summer so much beauty
A simple friendship with a flower
Packed into a shining hour.

The teasel *(opposite)* is a tall plant that defends itself with
hooked prickles against grazing beasts without deterring
the butterflies. *Above*: a Red Admiral on Michaelmas
Daisies.

FOR OLD TIME'S SAKE

Think golden thoughts
And send out gentle blessings
Offer a prayer
Each time you look above.

For kindly people
Found in pleasant places
Remember them, for old time's sake
With love.

This lovely bridge, spanning the River Cam at Cambridge, belongs to Clare College. It dates from 1640; the college itself was founded in 1326.

Published and Printed in Great Britain by Jarrold & Sons Ltd, Norwich
85306 231 5   © *Jarrold & Sons Ltd, Norwich* 273